TRASH

Kaye Umansky

Illustrated by Judy Brown

PUFFIN BOOKS

This book is dedicated to my good friend,
Eugene Manzi, whose help in preparing it has been
absolutely useless!

PUFFIN BOOKS

Published by the Penguin Group
Penguin Books Ltd, 27 Wrights Lane, London W8 5TZ, England
Viking Penguin, a division of Penguin Books USA Inc.
375 Hudson Street, New York, New York 10014, USA
Penguin Books Australia Ltd, Ringwood, Victoria, Australia
Penguin Books Canada Ltd, 2801 John Street, Markham, Ontario, Canada L3R 1B4
Penguin Books (NZ) Ltd, 182–190 Wairau Road, Auckland 10, New Zealand

Penguin Books Ltd, Registered Offices: Harmondsworth, Middlesex, England

First published 1991
1 3 5 7 9 10 8 6 4 2

Text copyright © Kaye Umansky, 1991
Illustrations copyright © Judy Brown, 1991
All rights reserved

The moral right of the author and illustrator has been asserted

Set in Gill on Apple Macintosh Desk Top Publishing system by
Clare Truscott Design, London

Printed in Great Britain by Clays Ltd, St Ives plc

FROM THE EDITOR

Hi there!   pop fans ☑
teeny boppers ☐
wannabes ☐
rockers ☐
dudes ☐
rappers ☐
others ☐   (tick which one applies to you)

Welcome to *Trash Hits* – the pop magazine that gives you the low-down on some of the most rubbishy bands around. Meet the stars that have made it to the bottom: The Dull (the most *boring* band in the world), The Teachers (the *strictest* band in school), The Cutesy Pies (the *yuckiest* band in the sweetshop), Kit Spitt and the Gitts (the band you'd *least* like to spend a wet playtime with), Sandra and the Snitches (say no more), The Dinner Ladies (the *cleanest* hands in the business) and many more.

Meet Wayne Swankpot and find out how he manages to look so gorgeous and stay so modest. Test yourself with the *Trash Hits* quiz to see if *you too* could become a megastar and learn the lyrics of such trashy songs as 'Warmed-up Wellies', 'Telling the Teacher on You' and 'Please Don't Step on My Brown Lace-up Shoes'.

There are instruments to make, T-shirts to send off for, horoscopes to read, a problem page and an hilarious A to Z of pop music in this first (and definitely the last) issue of *Trash* (Hip, hip, hurray) *Hits*.

Yeah!

☑ WISIWYG (what I say is what you get) JONES Editor
☐ ED.E. TORR Editor

                                 (tick which one you prefer)

EDITORIAL TEAM

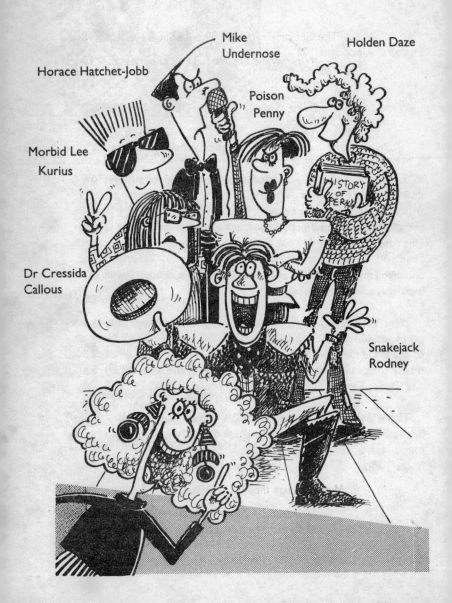

Horace Hatchet-Jobb

Mike Undernose

Holden Daze

Poison Penny

Morbid Lee Kurius

Dr Cressida Callous

Snakejack Rodney

FEATURES

SONG LYRICS

SHARP SHADES!

GIVE YOUR EYES THE COMFORT AND PROTECTION THEY DESERVE AND CHOOSE FROM OUR RANGE OF EVER SO COOL AND GROOVY SUNGLASSES.

Each pair comes with a mirror so you can admire yourself and a set of ear-plugs so you can't hear people jeering when you bang into lamp-posts and trip over pieces of fluff, etc.

THE CHARTS: TRASH HITS' TOP 25 SINGLES

1 Warmed-up Wellies
The Dinner Ladies (Roastbeef)

2 I Love Me
Wayne Swankpot (Bigtime Records)

3 Smashing the Place Up
The Shocking Baddies (Rough House)

4 Remember My Name
Thingy and the Other One (Yawn)

5 Hate! Grrrrr! Shut Up!
Kit Spitt and the Gitts (Cross Records)

6 We're So Cute
The Cutesy Pies (Yuck)

7 Blown Away
Augusta Wind and Gail Forcewarning (Breeze Records)

8 Groovin' With the Gravy
The Plumps (Roastbeef)

9 Do Ya Want Your Hair Pulled?
Beryl and the Big Girls (Rough House)

10 Please Don't Step on My Brown Lace-up Shoes
The Dull (Yawn)

11 No One Cares
The Complainers (Kleenex Records)

12 Outa My Way!
Bibi Beep and the Honkers (Roadhog)

WINDOW ON THE STARS

The Dinner Ladies

LUNCHTIME (An in-depth study by our roving investigative reporter, Mike Undernose.)

OK. So. What do we make of the sudden rocketing to fame of The Dinner Ladies? Their single, 'Warmed-up Wellies', has been the surprise trash hit of the year. The follow-up, 'Have You Washed Your Hands?', has just been released and is currently racing up the charts. The kids are starting to dress like them. The word's out that flowered nylon overalls are in. It's fashionable to have flour on your hands. Yes, The Dinner Ladies have certainly captured our imaginations.

So, who are they? What is the secret of their success? I was determined to meet Florence, Lil, Betty and Vera and find out for myself. Excitedly, I took myself along to St Brat's, Urchin Hill, where I knew the ladies would be about to serve up. As I made my way across the playground, I was bitten by an infant and knocked over by the caretaker's dog. It was a typical school.

When I finally found the head teacher's office, she made me write a hundred lines saying 'I Will Arrive On Time'. After I'd handed them in, I was allowed to go along to the hall, where The Dinner Ladies were just serving up. I knew it was lunchtime by the screams and the flying peas.

To my horror, I was force-fed cabbage and lumpy custard and had to conduct my interview in a queue with three hundred screeching children who, under pretence of asking for seconds, stole my tape recorder and broke all my pencils. So the following interview was the best I could do under very trying circumstances.

ME: Has your success come as a surprise to you?

FLORENCE: Have you washed your hands? Don't look like it.

LIL: 'E's askin' about our success, Flo. 'E wants to know if it's come as a surprise. No, course it ain't, you cheeky little blighter. We always knew we 'ad what it takes, didn't we, girls? Stop shovin', Jimmy Beard, and wait your turn.

ME: When did you first start singing together?

BETTY: What's wrong with that magic little word, then?

ME: When did you first start singing together, *please*?

VERA: Over the washin' up. We've always enjoyed a good sing song. I hope you're not leaving that cabbage, young man. Makes you see in the dark, cabbage.

ME: I thought it was carrots.

VERA: Are you arguing with me?

FLORENCE: *Hold everythin'!* We run out of spam. Joanna Sugden, stop pickin' your nose, girl, and run along to the kitchen. Tell cook we run out of spam.

ME: Which one of you wrote 'Warmed-up Wellies'?

BETTY: It were a team effort, weren't it, girls? We got the idea when Vera 'ere stuck 'er boots in the oven to dry out, an' we served 'em up by mistake. Wiv chips. The kids never even noticed. We 'ad a good laugh about it, I can tell you.

ME: Tell me about your image.

FLORENCE: Rubber gloves and aprons.

LIL: And a nice perm.

FLORENCE: Speak for yourself. Praise be! Here's the spam.

ME: What do you intend to do with the money you'll make from the single?

BETTY: Oh, buy a microwave. Definitely. And a dishwasher.

FLORENCE: New aprons and rubber gloves all round.

VERA: We'll probably give ourselves a rise.

LIL: We're thinkin' of buyin' one o' them new Stodgemaker machines. We spends most of our time makin' stodge. If we had one o' them Stodgemakers we'd do less cookin' an' 'ave more time for recordin' and that. Right, who's for seconds? No pushin'!

I am mown down by a howling mob of children, all brandishing forks. I crawl out hastily. Before I can make it, I am caught by the head teacher again, who makes me write another one hundred lines and take the guinea-pig home for the weekend.

HAPPENIN' OVERALLS!

Flowery overalls are in –
and that's official!

Team with a funky pair
of rubber gloves for
ultimate style!

No wardrobe is complete
this year without an
overall. Transform the stark
simplicity of a wool cardi
with this witty fashion
statement. Great
grooming! Chic,
snappy and neat.
A glamorous look
for both kitchen
and stage!

Available in durable
nylon or the rich easy
elegance of flannelette!

Choose from 3 super
designs –
Sunset in Egg
Hint of Sprout
Study in Gravy

£125.99 plus postage

News flash

Shriek! How about this, all you Dinner Ladies fans! The girls have released their new single, 'Have You Washed Your Hands?'. Taken from their Who's For Seconds? album, it's backed with the previously unreleased 'Where's Your Manners?' while the 12-inch also contains another new song, 'Twelve Green Bluebottles'. The Dinner Ladies are entering into negotiations over the proposed release of several tracks recorded live from St Brat's last Friday over the washing up. A spokesman for their current label, Roastbeef, said that the tracks were 'wonderful, with a particularly thrilling version of "My Way".'

'WARMED-UP WELLIES'

(The Dinner Ladies)
(To the tune of 'John Brown's Body')

Warmed-up wellies are the latest thing to eat,
They're nutritious and delicious with a subtle hint of feet,
Just serve 'em up with gravy as a substitute for meat
And they'll both go down a treat.

Chorus
Have a bite of warmed-up welly,
Guaranteed to warm your belly,
Advertised upon the telly,
They're just the job for me.

Warmed-up wellies are such chompy things to chew,
They're rubbery and blubbery and very good for you,
They're lubbery in a casserole or even in a stew
Or a welly vindaloo!

Chorus
Have a bite of warmed-up welly, etc.

15

Quiz

So you want to be a famous pop star. Here's a suitability test. Put a
tick in the box of your choice.

1. The right stage-name is important. Your name is Alfred Chest-
Pimple and you want to change it. Which of the following would you
choose:

- ☑ a. Flash Flamenco-dancing
- ☐ b. Rumplestiltskin
- ☐ c. Keith Adenoid
- ☑ d. I haven't a clue

2. Likewise, if your name is Gladys Piggy, would you change it to:

- ☐ a. Gabriella von Ritzitiara
- ☑ b. Natasha Nokabuttockoff
- ☐ c. Mrs Rowena Boat
- ☑ d. Dunno

3. Which of the following band names are the most hip and swinging:

- ☐ a. The Hip Replacements
- ☐ b. The Buttered Muffins
- ☐ c. The Rolling Pins
- ☑ d. Couldn't Care Less

4. Which of the following instruments do you consider essential:

- ☑ a. Outer Pangolian chin harp
- ☐ b. A dentist's drill
- ☐ c. A hoover
- ☐ d. I give in

5. More band names. Which of these do you prefer:

- ☐ a. Mega Nasty Thrash featuring The Destroying Savage Ogres
    From Outer Space
- ☐ b. Harry Tosis and the Toothpicks
- ☑ c. The Crumblies
- ☐ d. I'm clueless and always pick d

6. Your moment of glory has arrived. You run on stage, waving to an adoring audience of thousands. Will you be wearing:

☐ a. A pink tutu
☐ b. School uniform
☑ c. A gorilla costume
☑ d. Haven't the foggiest

7. Here is the verse of a song. You have to supply the last line. Tick the one you think most appropriate.
Ooooooh baby I'm your man,
Ooooooooh baby I'm your man,
Please come on home

☐ a. And you can meet my gran
☑ b. I'll drive you in the van
☐ c. And have a slice of flan
☐ d. Wot?

YOUR SUITABILITY RATING

Mostly ds:
Congratulations. Your casually indifferent attitude suggests that you are definitely pop star material. Please can I have your autograph?

Mostly Cs:
Hmm. Well, you'd need to work at it. Are you sure you really want to? There's only one way to find out. Buy yourself a guitar and some unusual trousers, book the Albert Hall for your first concert, invite all your mates and see how you get on. Best to be sure whether or not it's for you before going too far.

Mostly bs:
You stand slightly more chance. About as much as you have of becoming a brain surgeon in three easy lessons.

Mostly as:
Sorry. It's tough, I know, but you'll never make a pop star. However, don't despair. There is sure to be a niche for you somewhere. Why not try running away to Canada and becoming a lumberjack? Or, have you considered going to night school and learning to paint garden gnomes for a living? No? Me neither.

GREAT POP STARS OF OUR TIME:
The Dull

by Morbid Lee Kurius

Brian Boring
– lead vocals

Clifford Mundane
– drums

Dave Drab
– piano

Eric Stuffy
– bass

The Dull first met in Miss Killjoy's class at Dreary Street Comprehensive. Success has not gone to their heads, and they are much too sensible to give up their Saturday jobs. Brian works part-time in his gran's woolshop. Dave puts paper-clips in boxes. Eric edits the *Slug Fanciers' Weekly*. Clifford is a paper bag salesman. They all find their jobs 'all right'. In a recent survey, The Dull won the coveted title of 'Most Boring Band in the Universe'. A CROSS-SECTION* of the public was asked the following question:

Q: Which would you sooner do, watch a plank warp or listen to The Dull?

A GOOD-TEMPERED* section of the public was asked the same question. An overwhelming 98 per cent said they would take the plank any day. The remaining 2 per cent were Dull fans.

* Joke – geddit?

The Dull Interview

I interviewed The Dull in their favourite spot – a doctor's waiting-room. They go there every day to sit in silence and read old gardening magazines.

Q: Let's talk about fashion. Are you image conscious?

BRIAN: Oh yes, very. We have a band uniform. Grey knitted woollies and grey corduroy trousers with sensible shoes.

DAVE: Nylon anoraks in cold weather. With a nice warm scarf, probably brown. Or grey.

CLIFFORD: It helps to wear horn-rimmed glasses.

ERIC: Not true, Clifford. Some people who wear horn-rimmed glasses are very exciting.

CLIFFORD: That's true, Eric. We don't want their sort.

DAVE: A Dull haircut's essential, of course. We all have the same style. Brian's gran cuts it for us. She knits our grey jumpers too.

Q: What are your hobbies?

BRIAN: Listening to talks on the radio in Dutch. That's a Dull thing to do.

Q: Oh, you speak Dutch, do you?

BRIAN: No. That would make it interesting, wouldn't it?

DAVE: Sometimes I copy out the dictionary. I'm up to C.

CLIFFORD: I quite like knitting. Brian's gran's teaching me. I only use grey wool.

ERIC: Just sitting in waiting-rooms, really. Dreaming of the day I'll be old enough to retire and get the slug farm. Oh, happy day. . .

Q: Do you get a lot of fan mail?

BRIAN: Oh, yes. Long boring letters, written in small, neat writing. Dull fans write a lot, but they don't come and see us much. They prefer to spend a quiet evening at home in front of the telly, watching documentaries about concrete. So Dull gigs tend to be quiet affairs.

Q: Have you ever had an exciting gig?

ERIC: No. Oh yes, wait a minute. Remember the bank managers' reunion, lads? Clifford's pink tie caused a riot. It wasn't Dull enough, see. The fans pelted us with briefcases. Clifford got poked with a biro . . .

Q: Zzzzzzzzzzz

Albums

Dull (Yawn Records)

Deadly Dull (Yawn)

Shopping for Grey Corduroy Trousers (Yawn)

Shopping for Another Identical Pair of Grey Corduroy Trousers (Yawn)

Singles

'Please Don't Step on My Brown Lace-up Shoes' (Yawn)

'Do Wah Diddy Dull' (Tedious Records)

'My Baby Is an Accountant' (Monotone Records)

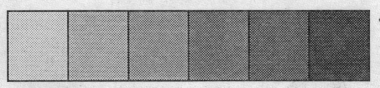

News flash

The Dull are working on a new album – which they claim should 'bore everyone comatose' – for release this year. In collaboration with producers Pipe and Slippers, the boys have so far recorded the following tracks: 'Maths Homework', 'Business Meetings', 'Waiting for the 14a Bus' and 'Let's Stay in and Stare at the Wall'.

Brian Boring, lead vocals, said this week: 'Yes, we're pleased with it. It's a typical Dull record. Our fans won't be disappointed.'

'PLEASE DON'T STEP ON MY BROWN LACE-UP SHOES' **– THE WORDS**

You can pull my tie,
Muss my hair
Pull my sleeve, but don't you dare to
Step on, step on my brown lace-up shoes,
You can do anything, but don't
Step on my brown lace-up shoes (please).

When they wear out
It'll be a shame,
Guess I'll buy another pair the same,
Oh, don't you step on my brown lace-up shoes,
You can do anything, but don't
Step on my brown lace-up shoes (please).

Chorus
Please don't, please don't,
Please don't, please don't
Shoes, oh my shoes,
do be careful, etc.

23

Reviews

This week's singles
are reviewed by our
two meanest critics,
Poison Penny and
Horace Hatchet-Jobb.

Noddy and Big-Ears
'Riding in My Little Yellow Car' (Toytown)

Dreadful stuff. We particularly disliked the
squeaky backing vocals by The Dollies, and
Mr Wobbly Man's guitar solo was pathetic.
Noddy's jingling hat-bell got on our nerves.
Big-Ears can't sing. A miss.

The Complainers
'Cheesed Off '(Kleenex)

Well. What do you expect from the boys
who gave us 'Fed Up, More Fed Up and
Still Fed Up'? If all your friends hate you
and your pocket money's been stopped
and you're in bed with flu being forced to
eat cold cauliflower against your will while
simultaneously writing a hundred thank-you
letters, you will find this LP hugely
enjoyable. We didn't. A miss.

Lord Nelson
A Selection of Sailing Songs Live from Trafalgar Square With the Pigeon Fanciers' Symphony Orchestra
(Old Hat)

Hmm. A golden oldie. Trouble is, Nelson never really moves with the times. Come to think of it, he never moves at all. He's stood still for years. It's time we had some new music. And 'Dead from Trafalgar Square' would be a more honest description. Another miss.

The Three Bears
'Hey! You! Get Offa My Chair!'
(Bruin Records)

Oh, really! It's time The Three Bears came up with something new. They've already brought out *'Who's Been Sleeping in My Bed'* and *'No Porridge Today'*. What's with this Goldilocks stuff? Don't they ever talk about anything else? A miss.

Maggie T
'My Old Sweet Self' (Blue Tone Records)

Poor old Maggie T. She keeps on churning out the same old stuff, but nobody's buying it. What a pity. A miss.

The Three Little Pigs
'Do the Chinny Chin Chin' (Oink)

Oh no! Yet more of this fairy tale stuff! It's time the pigs stopped producing this slop and got out of the sty into the real world. All right, so it'll do well in the discos once everybody's mastered the steps, but let's face it, these endless pig songs get wildly boaring.

The Shocking Baddies

LENNY'S MUM BANS HIM FROM PLAYING!

'I AM AN ANIMAL!' says Lenny Lout.

'When I play on stage I am like a wild animal,' says Lenny Lout, lead singer with the Shocking Baddies. 'I just can't help it. It's like this compulsive urge to break things and use naughty words.'

The above quote has caused a lot of trouble for Lenny. He has received loads of letters from the animal rights people, complaining that he is giving wild animals a bad name. A spokesman said: 'We challenge him to produce a single swearing squirrel who throws television sets from hotel windows.'

Even worse, Lenny's mum, Mrs Lout, read it. She says she's had enough of his nonsense and she's keeping him in until he learns how to behave. That just leaves Kev (drums), Trev (bass) and Nev (lead guitar). Lenny doesn't know it, but in his absence Kev, Trev and Nev are planning to fire him. But when it comes to it, they'll probably chicken out, because he's the only one whose uncle's got a motor bike.

ALBUMS

**The Shocking Baddies
(Rough House)
Rude, Ill-mannered and Cheeky
(Rough House)
Yob (Hooligan Sounds)**

SINGLES

**'Smashing the Place Up' (Rough House)
'Sorry About Smashing the Place Up'
(Sheepish Records)**

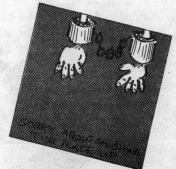

FASHION

**What the ultimate heavy metal
fan is wearing**

A super manhole cover
by Wandsworth Council

Awful old leather
jacket from
Rip-off
Mail Order

Loo chains,
towel rings and
other bathroom
accessories from
a selection at Lav's,
Covent Garden

Spray-on
trousers
by Yukki

Boots from
A Skip

THE HEAVY METAL PAGES

29

SHOCKING TOYS

Heavy metal fans get younger all the time. For this reason, Nasty-Price Toys Inc. have designed a super new range of toys suitable for all the nappy-wearing metal fans out there. Just look at our great selection!

Laughing Skull
(wind it up and it bites your finger!)
£26.99

Two-tone Musical Guillotine (plays 'Jingle Bells'. Doubles as potty) £35

Pop-up Frenzied Werewolf
(a great favourite)
£19.99

Chattering Vampire Teeth
(press a button, and these cute teeth go for the throat. Hours of amusement) £18.99

Haunted Wendy House
(durable plastic. Free bucket of ectoplasm) £An arm and a leg

Pushalong Tinkletonk Snarling Crocodile
(for those first faltering steps) £57.99

Play and Learn Axe
(not recommended for under 3s) £12.99

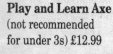

Build and Destroy Activity Pack
(more hours of fun) £23.99

Readers' Letters and Tips

Dear *Trash Hits*,
I have a complaint. How dare that idiot Morbid Lee Kurius write all that stuff the other week about us Complainers fans, making out we're always complaining and that. What right has he to call us (I quote) 'a bunch of miserable twits who just like to burble on about how everything's unfair and it's time somebody did something.'
How grossly unfair. Personally, I think it's time somebody did something.

Disgusted Complainers Fan,
Stonehenge

Dear *Trash Hits*,
Someone told me you can buy a personalized, iced, three-tier cake emblazoned with the fabulous Dinner Ladies autographs for a mere £48.53. Is this true? Please give details. I am inquiring for a friend.

Greedy Pig, Leeds

Trash Hits replies:
No, it is not true. You are the victim of a misprint. It is not a cake, it is a roly-poly pudding. It costs £148.53. The autographs are extra. And they're sold out anyway. So there.

Dear *Trash Hits*,
I knew The Dribbles when they were mere Slurps – and believe you me, they were much better then.

Mrs Cecilia Sloshy

Trash Hits replies:
A copy of The Dribbles' latest single, 'Dance the Salivation', is even now not on its way to Mrs Sloshy for her interesting observation.

Dear *Trash Hits*,
Have any of your readers got 'Deep Sea Blues' by The Snorkels? I am anxious to get hold of a copy to make up the set. I already have

'Down Under' by The Flippers and the great Aqua Lung's version of 'Breathless'.

Coral Reef, Australia

Trash Hits replies:
Yes, we've got it. But don't hold your breath, cos we're not giving it to you.

Dear *Trash Hits*,
I have just discovered the most amazing thing. If you take the first letters from the words Duster, Underpass, Lump and Lifeless, you get DULL. Don't faint.

Brian Bonkers, Berks.

Trash Hits replies:
You are obviously two bananas short of a fruit bowl. Go and see your doctor immediately.

Dear *Trash Hits*,
All our family are fans of Thingy and the Other One. My daughter, Wochamecallit, thinks they are just great. So does Wossisname, my son. Even Oojamaflip, my wife, thinks they are great.

Terry Bull-Fawnames,
Amnesia Avenue, You-Know-
That-Big-Continent-Where-
The-Kangaroos-Live

Trash Hits replies:
Sorry, we were going to say something about the thingamy but we forgot what.

Dear *Trash Hits*,
What an amazingly wonderful, staggeringly brilliant magazine! Quite the best read I have ever had in my life. And so well informed. I cannot believe how anyone could ever buy another rival magazine if they could have *Trash Hits*. Congratulations to you all.

Satisfied customer

PS Please leave the bag of used £5 notes in the stump of the old oak tree as promised.

Dear *Trash Hits*,
I think I may have a talent for writing romantic ballads about love and stuff and I would be glad of your opinion. I enclose a sample of one of my songs. Feel free to show it to any famous pop stars. It's called 'Ooooh Baby Ooooh'. Ahem.

Ooooh baby ooooh
I love youuuuuu
Love me toooooo
Or I'll feel so red.

I feel the last line maybe needs a little more work, what do you think?

Hopeful songwriter, Kent

Trash Hits replies:
You will never make a romantic ballad writer. All romantic ballads must by law include the words moon and June. Your pathetic effort had neither. Go to the back of the orchestra.

Dear *Trash Hits,*
I can dance the Salivation, and I've got photographs to prove it.

Mrs Ava Kneesup, St Austel

Trash Hits replies: She has too.

Dear *Trash Hits,*
At a recent Dribbles concert in Birmingham, I bought two cans of Burpo, four packets of crisps, three chocolate bars and a packet of fruit gums. I was horrified to be charged a staggering £2.17. The identical items could have been bought in my local supermarket for a mere £2.15. It quite spoiled my enjoyment of the concert.

Ms Irma Skinflint, Plymouth

Dear *Trash Hits,*
Who wrote Oliver Twist?

Book Worm

Trash Hits replies:
How the Dickens should we know?

MUSICAL TIP OF THE WEEK

Mrs Compost of Sheffield wins this week's fiver.

Keep your records in perfect condition by never playing them! Simply bring them home from the shop and place them, still in their jackets, on a high shelf. I have used this method for many years and never cease to be amazed by the results.

GENERAL TIP OF THE WEEK

Keep soap handy by storing it in the bathroom. I keep mine on the sink.

Mrs Winifred Batty, Shrops.

WRITERS' TIP OF THE WEEK

With the price of pencils today, it is as well to economize. Get one free by borrowing a friend's and breaking it in half.

L.Ed Toole, Grimsby

Your Very Own Personal File

All right, so you scored high in the quiz, and now you are a famous pop star. How will you know you have 'arrived'? Easy.

① Your eyes will suddenly become weak and you will have to wear sunglasses all the time on doctor's orders.

② All your jumpers will mysteriously grow shoulder-pads.

③ You will feel strangely compelled to rush off and get a silly haircut and spend thousands of pounds on new shoes.

④ You will swank around the place, talking about studios and albums and 'going on the road' and your image and so on.

⑤ You will become terribly spoilt and demanding, i.e. ordering people to go out and fetch you a bucket of caviare, three cheese rolls and a packet of jelly babies every two seconds.

⑥ You will be mobbed by screaming fans, all demanding bits of you to take home and weep over.

At this point, reporters from trendy magazines such as Trash Hits will pester you for interesting facts about yourself. They will ask you questions about potty-training and your favourite insect and so on. This is fun at first, but gets to be a drag after a while. Save yourself a lot of bother by filling in this personal file and handing it out wherever you go.

Full name Chris Liz Upana

Stage-name Minges

Address for fan mail The Palace

London (Buckingham)

Date of birth 2.11.82

If you're thinking of sending me a birthday present,

I would like horse and clothes

and ~~socks~~ shoes or maybe cd player (stereo)

On no account send me Mum I've got one

If you want to phone me, my number is 0208 872648

but I only accept flattering calls

I weigh an ideal (fuck knows) kilograms

I am a magnificent 2 centimetres tall

My eyes are (dotted, brown, pink, square, etc.) green

My ears are (big, floppy, etc.). ears

My mouth is (a talking point, usually full, etc.) a mouth

My hair looks like this (draw):

My noble nose is (describe in less than ten words)
pig like

35

I have (tick appropriate boxes):

- ☐ A beautiful singing voice
- ☐ Rhythm, man
- ☐ Thick eyebrows
- ☐ A dazzling smile
- ☐ Sticky-out ears
- ☑ A lovely head of hair
- ☐ Incredible musical talent
- ☐ Glasses
- ☑ Freckles

- ☐ Dimples
- ☐ An unusual style of dancing
- ☐ Dandruff
- ☑ A bad temper
- ☑ A good memory for faces
- ☑ Ticklish feet
- ☐ One or more really long nail(s)
- ☐ Nice manners

I live in a (tick):

- ☐ Palace
- ☑ House
- ☐ Flat
- ☐ Cave
- ☐ Other (please specify) ....

- ☐ Five-star hotel
- ☐ Tree
- ☐ Caravan
- ☐ Igloo

with my:

- ☑ Mum
- ☑ Dad
- ☐ Gnome
- ☐ Manager

- ☐ Gran
- ☐ Pet boa constrictor, Toby
- ☐ Hamster
- ☐ Stick insect, Lawrence

My favourite food is Chinese and ....

and .... and sometimes chips

Don't ever give me liver , I hate it.

My favourite pet is (tick box):

- ☐ Mountain goat
- ☐ Gerbil
- ☐ Boa constrictor
- ☐ Other (please specify) ...... horse

- ☐ Hamster
- ☐ Stick insect

- ☐ I have one
- ☑ I don't have one, but I wish I had

My favourite instrument is ...... drums

☐ I can play one   ☑ I cannot play one

What I can play is a ...... recorder

My favourite colour is ...... Blue

because it reminds me of ...... Blue

My favourite TV programme is ...... sesame Street

because I like ...... Big Bird

My favourite sport is ...... Horse riding

☐ I am brilliant at it   ☐ I am useless

☑ I am quite good   (tick box)

My favourite band is ...... The Chipmunks

My favourite song is ...... Away in a manger

Sometimes I sing in the bath: ☑ Yes   ☐ No

If I wasn't a pop star, I would be a ...... prostetute

because ...... I like sex

and besides it is cushy and will make me loads of money.

Signature ...... Chipmunk

Date 15.1.96

37

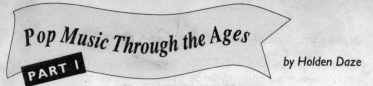

Pop Music Through the Ages
PART I
by Holden Daze

THE STONE AGE

Pop music began in the Stone Age. Not many people know that. But let us examine the evidence. We know for a fact that Stone Age people had clubs. We all know that pop music is played in clubs, right? There you are then.

[Ed: This is utterly pathetic. Who is this Holden Daze, and why is he working for this magazine?]

Some of you may think this is flimsy evidence.

[Ed. I most certainly do.]

Ah, but there's more. We know that cave-dwellers held rock concerts! With all those rocks around, it stands to reason. Today I bring you the truth about these ancient rites. Here are the answers to some of the questions I am always being asked.

Q: Why did Stone Age people play music?

A: In order to celebrate their good fortune, i.e. getting through a whole day without being eaten by a sabre-toothed tiger; finding a wild blackberry; catching a partially evolved lung-fish.

Q: Did a lot of Stone Age people get eaten by sabre-toothed tigers, then?

A: Oh, yes. It happened all the time. Particularly at night, when they were on their way to rock concerts.

Q: Where were the concerts held?

A: In damp, dark, festering caverns. Rather like today really.

Q: What was the music like?

A: Oh, the usual. The lyrics weren't up to much, but they got some nice rhythms going. People rattled tiger teeth and banged stones together. It was amazing what instruments they came up with, given a bone or two, a hollow log and a sack of gravel. Ug the Dischordant composed an entire Stone Age rock opera for five pieces of flint and an axe-head. Brilliant. You can still see the original instruments in the British Museum.

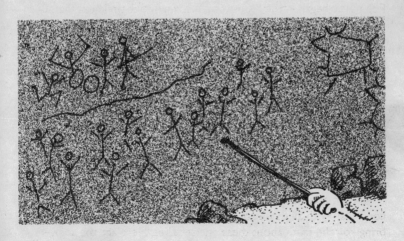

Q: What did pop stars wear, then? In those days?

A: Well, of course, the fashion scene was a bit primitive. What people wore depended mainly on what had died outside the cave. If it was a mammoth, the whole band wore matching woolly jumpers. But usually it was just rat skins. The odd bone through the nose, a feather or two. You know, anything that was lying around.

Q: Were refreshments provided at these 'rock concerts'?

A: Oh, yes. In the interval. Blackberry dip, barbecued lung-fish, devilled reptile. That sort of thing.

Q: What did these early rock stars drink?

A: Interesting you should ask that. Dr Fritz Von Nutt, the archaeologist, recently unearthed a sealed stone pot containing a potent beverage made of fermented blackberries and tiger doos.

Q: Did he taste it?

A: Yes, he tasted it.

Q: Well? What does he think?

A: You mean, what *did* he think!

Want to find out more? Simply fill in the coupon below and send me a tenner. I will happily send you a fact sheet.

✂ –

YES, HOLDEN! I WANT TO KNOW ALL ABOUT STONE AGE POP MUSIC AND HERE'S A TEN POUND NOTE.

Name ....

Address ....

....

[Ed. No more of this sort of thing, please.]

GREAT POP STARS OF OUR TIME:
The Cutesy Pies

by Morbid Lee Kurius

The Cutesy Pies consists of
Cherry, Cheryl and Charlene.
There was once a fourth
member, Shirley, but she
broke friends.

41

The Cutesy Pies were interviewed among two million cuddly toys in Charlene's bedroom, wearing the pink frilly frocks which have become their trademark.

Q: Don't you ever tire of being cute?

CHERRY: Tee, hee, hee. Ooooh, no. (Sucks thumb and giggles.)

CHERYL: We love it. (Nibbles a lolly prettily.)

CHARLENE: It'th thuch fun being cute. It duthn't matter if we forget the wordth or go out of tune. People jutht thay 'Oh, aren't they cute', which we are.
(Bats eyes, skips around a bit, twirls, cuddles teddy and looks wistful.)

Q: What's your greatest ambition?

CHERRY: To be a pwofessional bwidesmaid.

CHERYL: To have a doll named after me. Cindy, Barby, Cheryl.

CHARLENE: I want to thtar in a film where I die and become an angel and all the mumth cry a lot and thay 'Oh, ithn't she beautiful?'

Words to 'We're So Cute'

We got dimples, we got curls,
We're The Cutesy Pies,
Everyone likes little girls
With lovely big blue eyes . . .

(Sorry, readers. Rest of lyrics deleted on the advice of the Public Health Inspector, who warns that they will make you very sick, and are a serious health risk.)

ALBUMS

Buy This or I'll Hold My Bweath
(Simpering Sounds)

Sugar Treacle Candy
(Rowntree Records)

Songs for Swinging Bridesmaids
(Simpering Sounds)

SINGLES

'Mincey Wincey Spider'
(Yuck)

'We're So Cute'
(Yuck)

The Secrets of Wayne Swankpot's Beauty Routine

'I don't know what he does in that blooming bathroom,' says Wayne's mum. Well, here's her chance to find out. *Trash Hits* has finally persuaded Wayne Swankpot to reveal his morning beauty routine! What a scoop, eh? Read on if you wish to discover how Wayne sets about making himself the most wondrous human being to walk upon this planet. Imagine the scene. Wayne's bedroom. Mirrors everywhere. Walls papered with fan mail and posters of himself. Framed platinum discs. Bunches of flowers and opened boxes of chocolates sent by admiring fans. The alarm clock rings ....

7.30 Wake up, reach for hand-mirror I always keep by me. Examine myself at all angles. Yes, I am gorgeous. Even first thing in the morning. *Especially* first thing in the morning.

8.30 After looking at myself for an hour or so, I feel it is time to get up. I stretch my incredible body, wiggle my exquisite tootsies, flex my well-shaped ears, etc. Wow! Am I good looking or what?

8.35 Slip into my rare lugworm dressing-gown. I am very fond of this. It was given to me by a fan, and is made from a revolutionary new fabric woven by Tibetan monks from lugworm spit. Apparently the lugworms only produce a thimbleful of spit every six months, so there aren't many dressing-gowns like mine. Spend twenty-five enjoyable minutes posing in this incredible fashion statement before a full-length mirror.

9.00 Enough fun. Time now to get serious. Enter bathroom. Throw out anyone found in there, e.g. younger brother/sister/dog/old man with long white beard and sack, etc. Firmly close door, ignoring cries of protest from family. Examine profile from all angles in magnifying mirror. I am truly awesome. There is no other word. Yes there is. Phenomenal. That's a good one. And that's what I am.

9.05 Exercises first. So important to keep fit. I find that five minutes of vigorous hair combing followed by five minutes of moody pouting keeps me trim. Occasionally I do a bit of spot squeezing, which helps strengthen the fingers. Oh, and the odd session of posing on the exercise bike.

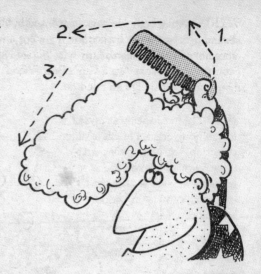

9.15 Oh-oh. How dreary. Someone is hammering at the bathroom door. Unbelievable. You'd think they'd be grateful to have a pop star in the family. Best ignore it. I run both bath taps at full force while running my eyes along the shelves which hold my various beauty preparations. Which bath oil shall it be today? *Strong 'n' Silent? Mean 'n' Moody? Smooth 'n' Sultry? Mr Hunk? Ladida?* It is a difficult decision. Finally I go for a particular favourite – the delicious *Eau de Big Head*, which suits me so well. Pour in large helping.

9.25 Step in bath. Lie back in scented bubbles and start singing. I love to practise in the bathroom, my voice always sounds so incredible. I run through all my hits. 'I Love Me', 'I, Who Have Everything', 'Mirrors Are a Guy's Best Friend', 'I'm So Vain', and many more. Gosh, I'm so talented.

9.45 Yet more hammering at door. Continue to ignore it. Make mental note to order some more of my favourite talcum powder, Explosion in a Garden Centre. I'm down to my last barrel and would hate to run out.

10.00 The door is nearly down. I step from bath and towel myself dry in leisurely fashion. Reach for hair mousse . . .

Sadly, Wayne was unable to continue. At this point, the bathroom door burst open and he was savagely attacked by his loving family who messed his hair up, threw away his soap-on-a-rope collection and broke three of his combs.

News flash

Wayne Swankpot has added another London date to his current tour. He will be appearing at El Snobbo's, Camden Town. In order to qualify for tickets, you must know somebody in the royal family, or even better, someone who can get a discount at Boots.

SPECIAL OFFER TO READERS OF TRASH HITS!

Free! Three – yes, THREE of our best-selling skin products! We don't waste money on fancy packaging. We don't hold with fancy pots and jars. We just dollop the stuff in brown paper bags and hope for the best. That's why everything's dirt cheap.

Greaseball Zit Cream A super-effective course of grease treatment for your skin. Popular with pop stars, royalty and car mechanics. Five generous dollops for the price of one. **Only £8.99.**

Oriental Wash 'n' Grind Pore Grains

For centuries, the Chinese have regarded bits of grit suspended in mud as one of nature's cleansing agents. At least, we think that's what they said, but we can't speak Chinese and could have got it wrong. **Buy 100 grains for just £15 and get one free!**

Len's Lizard Oil Remarkable cure-all from South America. Said to benefit those who suffer from acne, tiredness, ingrowing toe nails, hairy noses, stress, annoying relatives and lank, lack-lustre hair. Gargle with it three times a day or simply shampoo in.

 -

Send your mail order to:
'Orrible Oozy Zit Eruptions Research (OOZER)
I Sore Place, Musson Picket, Dorset

Please send me all these wonderful products without delay.

Name ....

Address ....

(Send no money now. Just send loads later.)

49

FIRST, THE DINNER LADIES, AND NOW...

The Teachers

(Another exclusive in-depth interview by your very own roving investigative reporter, Mike Undernose.)

★ **They're from St Brat's School!**

★ **They're the Next Big Thing!**

★ **They wrote the smash hit 'Stay in at Playtime' during a staff meeting one Tuesday lunchtime.**

★ **They're The Teachers!**

Yes, folks, at last I can bring you news of the rapid rise to stardom of the latest all-singing, all-dancing, amazing pop sensation to have burst forth from St Brat's!

So. Who are they? What is the secret of their success? I was determined to meet The Teachers and find out for myself. The group consists of five members: Mr Fogpatch (Art, vocals and guitar); Miss Chalk (Biology and drums); Mr Sprinter (Football and tambourine); Ms Birch (Creative writing and trumpet); and, of course, we mustn't forget dear old Mrs Woolly (Extra Reading Practice and kazoo).

Excitedly and with bated breath, I once again entered St Brat's — scene of my historic meeting with The Dinner Ladies. After much creeping around corridors, I finally located The Teachers in the staffroom half buried among piles of books for marking, dirty old coffee cups and packets of digestive biscuits. I asked them why they wanted to be pop stars when they had such a super job already.

'After the success of The Dinner Ladies, we thought we might as well have a go,' explained Mr Fogpatch. 'By the way, I didn't hear a knock before you walked in. Go out and come in again properly.'

'We intend to be the brainiest band in pop,' explained Miss Chalk. 'We also think we're going to be very popular, especially among the pupils in our school. If they don't buy our records, we double their homework. Easy as pie, really.'

'If that doesn't do the trick, we can always cancel swimming and set daily spelling tests,' agreed Ms Birch with an evil chuckle.

'A hundred press-ups,' added Mr Sprinter.

'Well, I shall ask them nicely,' announced dear old Mrs Woolly. 'Have a digestive biscuit, lovey,' she urged me.

The Teachers are renowned for their trendy image, which usually involves strange, sticking up hair styles, mad eye-rolling and muttering under the breath. I wasn't sure the look would 'catch on', and said so, as tactfully as I could. They seemed a little hurt by my comments, and there was talk of making me stay after school to tackyback the library books. So I changed the subject.

I commented on the special effects used in their brilliant video of 'Stay in at Playtime'.

'Chalk dust,' explained Mr Fogpatch. 'There's a bit in the song where we all run across the playground in slow motion with our arms open, and we wanted this misty effect. So we got Class 4 to throw a few sacks of chalk dust around.'

'I loved making the video,' sighed Miss Chalk. 'I think it's great. I make my class watch it at least nine times a day. I think it will stay in all our memories for a long time, don't you, Mrs Woolly?'

'Oh, it will, lovey, it will,' agreed Mrs Woolly, giving me a little wink and handing over a Jammy Dodger.

Sadly, I never got it. The bell rang, the washing-up monitors appeared and The Teachers snatched up their whips and ran into their classrooms. And me? I was forced to join the choir and stay after four o'clock for woodwork class. Anyone need a pipe-rack?

REVIEW

VIDEO – THE TEACHERS – 'STAY IN AT PLAYTIME'

'A super video, bags of chalk dust, loads of slow-motion running about . . .' – *Teacher* Magazine

'. . . Some unusual dancing from Ms Birch . . .' – Mrs Ava Kneesup

'. . . Quite an interesting netball match going on in the background . . .' – *Sportsperson*

'. . . Superb . . . Mrs Woolly has star quality . . .' – *Daily Rag*

Pop Music Through the Ages
PART 2
by Holden Daze

ROMAN TIMES

[Ed. I thought I said no more of this historical rubbish.]
Holden Daze – This is better. Really. Just one more chance.
[Ed: OK. But You Have Been Warned.]

I have received many letters from readers asking me about this fascinating period of pop history. Sadly, I do not have enough space to answer all their questions. But here are just a few.

Q: How was Roman society structured?

A: There were three distinct classes:

   1. Rich grape-eaters who wrote song lyrics and wore designer togas and went to trendy parties thrown by Caesar. (Caesar, of course, ran the music business, along with everything else.)

2. Foot soldiers and slaves.

3. Peasants under occupation.

Q: How come the foot soldiers didn't join a band?

A: You can't play guitar with your feet. Besides, they were always away on campaigns. Also they were tone-deaf.

Q: Didn't the slaves or the peasants ever celebrate?

A: Celebrate what?

Q: All right. Let's hear about Caesar's parties, then, where all this pop music got played. Why did the guests always lie down on cushions?

A: It was either that or falling down on a hard floor. Ever tried mead?

Q: Let's hear about the music.

A: The main spot was always a harp recital by Caesar. When he finished, the party guests got the slaves to make idiots of themselves, singing sad songs about their lot. Or they poked at peasants with sticks until they sang rustic melodies.

Q: What about food at these parties?

A: Say what you like about Caesar, he always did his guests proud. Typical Italian hospitality. An average do would have forty-three courses. Minestrone soup, boars' heads, roast swan, twelve different types of pasta, whole salmons, individual pizzas, and so on. The Romans were a greedy lot with a sweet tooth. It was common practice to sick up the starters and main courses to make room for the profiteroles . . .

[Ed. I'm sorry. I simply do not know what ancient Roman profiteroles are doing in an up-to-date magazine like Trash Hits. *Definitely no more.]*

Home-made Instruments

SAVE YOURSELF POUNDS!

A useful step-by-step guide for those of you who can't yet afford the real thing.

Calling all budding pop stars! Did you know that you can make your own musical instruments without having to spend a penny? Well, you can. Simply select the instrument of your choice from the following comprehensive list and follow our simple instructions.

Origami Electric Piano

① Get huge piece of paper.

❷ Fold along line AB.

③ Fold along line XY.

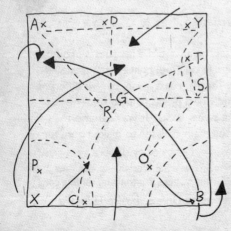

❹ You may need someone to help you with this. Connect RAC to CAR and RSPCA to DOG. Revolve 360° and tuck in both corners, taking care to overlap X so that BBC and ITV are in opposition to each other. Fold in half. Pull out corners to make legs. Does yours look like a piano? Neither does mine.

Drum

① Take a kettle.

② Find something to hit it with.

Voila! You have one kettledrum.

* Note: In deep dark forests where all the telephone kiosks have been vandalized and the postal service is notoriously unreliable, drums are used to send messages. When you play your home-made kettledrum, you too are sending a message to your neighbours. The message says 'I AM PLAYING MY DRUM AND I DO NOT CARE THAT YOU ARE SLEEPING.'

Do not be surprised if the neighbours react accordingly. Are you absolutely sure you want to be a drummer? Why not opt for something safer, like a triangle? Even better, an Hungarian ear flute.

Hungarian Ear Flute

① Hang an egg-slicer on your ear.

② Stand in front of a fan.

(It might not be an exact replica of the real Hungarian ear flute, but none of your friends will know that. Unless they're Hungarian.)

Papier Mâché Saxophone

① Ask all your friends to save up all their old newspapers.

② Hire a forklift truck and collect them.

③ Deposit newspapers in kitchen.

④ Tear up into a trillion little pieces.

⑤ Mix with flour and water until you have a generous amount of gloppy stuff.

⑥ Mould carefully into shape of saxophone.

⑦ Leave to dry overnight.

*Note: The following day, you can add all those important little details – like the holes, the valves, the gold paint, etc. Ask your mum or dad to help you with these.

Who Said What?

On the left is a list of amazing things pop stars have said. On the right is a list of pop stars. Can you match the pop star to the quote? Draw a nice line between them.

THE QUOTES

'I used to be conceited but now I'm perfect.'

'But I like putting paper-clips in bags . . .'

'Don't speak with your mouth full, Trevor, what would your mum say.'

'Short back and sides? Or would modom prefer a perm?'

'There's a shocking draught in here. And how come there aren't any sandwiches? My tea's cold . . .'

'Ozone layer. . . greenhouse effect . . . litter. . . acid rain . . .'

'Yahoo!'

'Of course, the whole purpose of making this embarrassing record is to show our kids up in front of their friends, ho, ho, ho.'

T H E ★ S T A R S

Lil Dinner Lady

Dave Drab of The Dull

Member of The Ecologically Sound

Wayne Swankpot

A Complainer

Roy Rodgers

A Hairdresser

Member of The Dads

Snakejack Rodney's Country Corner

Howdy, y'all! Yep, it's your ole pal, Snakejack Rodney, bringin' you the very latest in country sounds.

First, the noos y'all bin waitin' fer. Lil Orphant Annie's new single's out, ya hoo! It's called 'Ah Wuz Poorer'n You', and yes, folks, it brung tears to mah ahs. [Ed. My eyes.]

Ah talked to Lil Orphant Annie in her penthouse suite in the Loaded Texan Hotel, where she wuz havin' her curls glued on bah wun of her servants. She granted me fahve minutes of her tahm to tell me all about her heart-breakin' chilehood.

SNAKEJACK RODNEY: Howdy, lil sister, I heerd you had a plum dismal chilehood. Heerd you wuz reel poor. Care to tell us about it?

LITTLE ORPHANT ANNIE: Hey, bartender! Bring another crate of champagne! Oh, ah was poor all raht. We lived ten to a bed in an ole shack. Ah had no maw, a crazy drunk paw and nine brothers, all called John. Hey, buster! Make that two crates!

SNAKEJACK RODNEY: Any partickerler reason why they wuz all called John?

LITTLE ORPHANT ANNIE: I told yah. Paw wuz crazy. Hey! Somebody pop out and buy me another yacht. And while you're about it, get me a caviarburger with double cheese, double french fries, large side salad, large chocolate milkshake an' a slice of banana cream pie. Hey, what am I talkin' about? Don't mess about, just buy me the restaurant. What wuz I sayin'? Oh, yeah, we wuz so poor, we only had the one pair o' boots between us. Six-inch platforms, nobody'd wear 'em. Never had nothin' to eat 'cept fer stale crumbs. Picked cotton all day. Terrible.

SNAKEJACK RODNEY: You're makin' up fer it now though, aincha?

LITTLE ORPHANT ANNIE: OK, fella, that's your fahv minutes up. Hey, butch! Over here! Mah bodyguard'll show you out. Where in tarnation is that food?

★ ★ ★

The Words to 'Ah Wuz Poorer'n You'

Mah paw was a drunk an' mah maw had passed on,
An' ah had nine brothers who all were called John,
We worked pickin' cotton frum daylight til dusk
Fer a small hunk of cheese an' a mouldy ole crust.

Chorus
Yeah, ah wuz was poorer'n you
Ah was poorer'n you,
If you think you wuz poor, well don' think it no more
Cos ah wuz poorer'n you.

Our clothes wuz juss rags an' our feet they wuz bare,
We had one pair of boots which we took turns to share,
We had one piece of gum which we took turns to chew
And we used it on Sundays to flavour the stew.

Yeah, ah wuz poorer'n you. . . etc.

We lived by the side of an old railroad track,
Til a train came along and ran over our shack,
We stood by the ruins, we cried and we cried,
Then our faithful ole dawg juss keeled over'n died.

Yeah, ah wuz poorer'n you . . .

Snakejack Rodney's Country Style Fan Bag

Dear Snakejack,

I know you're an expert on cowboys. Here is my question. Whatever happened to the Lone Ranger? My mum says she used to fancy his horse. And what was his friend called?

Bronco Bessy

S.R. Well, Bessy, some believe that the daring masked rahder of the plain is still out there searchin' fer more thrills and adventures. Others say he's retired and runnin' a small hardware shop in Hull. His friend was called Pinta. Or was it Tintin? Or Poncho . . . ?

Dear Snakejack Rodney,

Can you settle an argument between me and my friend and tell me how much water a ten-gallon hat would hold?

Lassoo Lola

S.R. No.

Dear so-called Snakejack Rodney,

Are you a real cowboy, or is it true what my dad says, that you used to work behind the counter at Boots? He says he distinctly remembers purchasing a bottle of asprin and a hot-water bottle from you. By the way, the Lone Ranger's friend was Tonto.

Suspicious Know-All, Kent

S.R. Ain't no truth in this, pal. An' if your paw's the one who made all that fuss about his change, tell 'im go boil his head. And ah still think it wuz Tintin.

What's in Their Pockets?

We asked four pop stars to turn out their pockets. This is what we found.

LIL - DINNER LADY

A floor plan of a super kitchen.

Ancient family recipe for spiced sock pudding.

Smelly old floorcloth (for forcible washing of filthy hands).

Framed photo of grandchildren.

Fermenting jar of home-bottled jam.

Rubber gloves.

WAYNE SWANKPOT

A mirror to preen in (because he's so unspeakably vain).

Five combs.

Dental floss.

Nail file.

A fan letter saying how brilliant he is.

Bundles of five-pound notes (to show off with).

Spare pair of sunglasses.

ERIC STUFFY OF THE DULL

A book called *Training Your Slug* by Ernest Nutty.

A darning-needle and a small ball of grey wool (in case he needs to repair a small hole in his jumper any time).

Charity sticker for Save the Giant Javanese Tree Slug.

A piece of fluff.

Ten pence (which he is cautiously saving for a rainy day because he is so unutterably dull).

MS BIRCH OF THE TEACHERS

A pair of plastic lips (as playing the trumpet makes hers sore).

A set of brightly coloured letters with magnets on them (for creative writing).

A half-eaten digestive biscuit.

A cane *[Ed: no, surely not?]*

Chalk (for creating misty effects when on video).

The school bell.

A photo of 4B.

WAYNE SWANKPOT

by Morbid Lee Kurius

**The Complainers consists of
Des Content (whining vocals)
and Phil Forlorn (whinging violin).**

Desmond and Philip have had it tough. They claim that they are always being picked on, and they're probably right. They catch a lot of colds so their mums keep them in a lot. Both are spotty. Des looks silly in swimming-trunks, and Phil burns badly in the sun. Des is prone to boils, and Phil has this very high voice, which makes people laugh at him. The boys certainly have a lot to complain about.

Q: How would you describe your music?

PHIL: Just a minute. It's far too hot in here. Are you seriously expecting us to be interviewed under these conditions? I'm afraid we can't possibly say another word unless you install air-conditioning.

(*Trash Hits* arranged for air-conditioning to be installed immediately. Six months later, the interview continued.)

Q: How would you describe your music?

DES: Oh, depressing. Let's face it, we don't get played at parties much, do we, Phil?

PHIL: I wouldn't know. I've never been invited to one. Bit chilly in here, isn't it? You'd think they'd do something about that, wouldn't you?

DES: People play our records when they're doing their maths homework. Or if they're having an operation the next day. Or another spot's just come up.

PHIL: Or the cat's lost.

DES: Right. Dismal sorts of occasions.

Q: Have you always been miserable?

DES: These seats are hard, aren't they? I'm getting terrible back-ache. What did you say?

Q: Have you always been miserable?

DES: Oh, yes. We're heavily into self-pity, aren't we, Phil?

PHIL: It's what comes of being misunderstood.

DES: We formed The Complainers one Friday lunchtime. Someone threw my satchel over a wall, remember, Phil? And I lost my Snoopy pencil-box.

PHIL: And I was forced to take violin lessons against my will.

DES: We had a tough childhood.

PHIL: We sat down in the cloakroom and wrote our first song. It was called 'Fed Up Every Friday'.

DES (singing): We're cheesed off every Monday, and we're fed up Tuesday too . . .

PHIL: We're getting worse on Wednesday, and on Thursday, boy, we're blue!

DES: On Saturdays we're mopey . . .

PHIL: And on Sundays we are miz . . .

TOGETHER: But we're most fed up on Fridays and we don't know why that is.

DES (blowing nose): Beautiful, that. Right, that's it, time's up, end of interview, bring on the sandwiches. What d'you mean, no sandwiches? I distinctly remember being promised refreshments . . .

ALBUMS

Fed Up (Kleenex)

More Fed Up (Kleenex)

Still Fed Up (Kleenex)

SINGLES

'Why Bother?' (Nightmare)

'No One Cares' (Nightmare)

'Give Up' (Nightmare)

WORDS TO 'WHY BOTHER?'

Why bother? No one cares,
Why bother? Nothing's fair,
Why bother? All is dust,
Why bother? Nothing's just.

Chorus
Don't brush your teeth today,
They're sure to fall out anyway.

Dinner Of The Week

Every week we ask famous pop stars to tell us all about their favourite dinner. Our star guests this week are the experts themselves – the fabulous Dinner Ladies! They were 'tickled pink' that *Trash Hits* wanted them to choose Dinner of the Week. Lil, Florence, Betty and Vera hold rather old-fashioned views about school dinners. Here's what they have to say:

'We like good old stodge and plenty of it. Lots of grease, of course, and make sure you always ask for a tough cut of meat. Don't be afraid to experiment. If you can get away with an old shoe, it works out even cheaper.'

Wise words. So, here's The Dinner Ladies' choice. First, the main course.

SHOE PARMIGIANA

2 old tennis shoes, thinly sliced
1 tablespoon flour
1 finely ground egg
Salt and pepper
1 oz Cherry Blossom shoe
    polish (red if poss.)
1 litre old chip fat
finely chopped shoe-lace
pinch of oregano
sprig of parsley

METHOD

1. Flatten the shoe slices with rolling-pin or baseball bat. Season with salt and pepper, dip into flour. Fry in old chip fat. Leave to toughen overnight.
2. Mix everything else together.
3. Pour resultant slop over sliced shoes.
4. Dish out to ravenous children.

Shoe Parmigiana is delicious with old mashed potato, a small bruised apple, or a green side-table. This versatile dish can be served hot or cold, as a main course or starter, or to poison people.

To follow, why not try this scrumptious afters:

STRAWBERRY APRON SURPRISE

1 reasonably clean apron, pref. flowery
pattern, strings removed
1 tin golden syrup
8 tablespoons red jam
1 jar chocolate spread
2 bags sugar
Wild strawberries

METHOD
1. Roll out apron.
2. Take scissors, cut apron into bite-sized portions.
3. Take rest of ingredients and mix together to form a rich sauce, adding more sugar to taste.
4. Pour your sauce over your apron pieces, taking care that each piece is properly coated.

This dish should ideally be sprinkled with wild strawberries, but if you are fresh out of them, use whatever you can find lying around. Gravel, bath salts, a handful of bird seed – as long as it sprinkles, it'll do just fine. Serve with custard, and there you have it. Cheap, tasty and easy to prepare.

(We're asked sometimes why this dish is called Strawberry Apron Surprise. Well, the apron is the main ingredient. The surprise bit is what you use instead of the strawberries.)

Pop Music Through the Ages

PART 3

by Holden Daze

THΞ ΣGYPTIΔNS

[Ed. What's this doing here? I thought I said no more of these.]

Holden Daze – One more. Please. It's really good. It's all about the Egyptians. A lot of people think the Egyptians didn't have a music business, but they did, you know. I mean, it's obvious, isn't it? The pyramids were vast concert halls. Contrary to what most people think, they were not tombs at all. And the mummies are not, as previously thought, bandaged bodies. They were probably the bouncers, and that was their uniform. You see, you can tell the Egyptians were dead musical because of all the pictures of them with lutes and stuff . . .

[Ed. My office. Now. Bring your own strait-jacket.]

DESIGNER TRAINERS
STUMPUP

– The last word in expensive designer trainers. Never in the history of feet has there been anything like them.

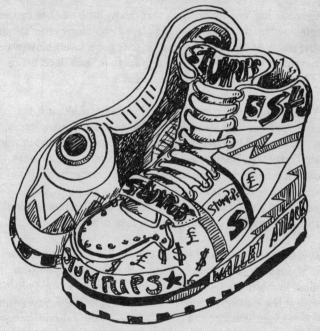

Stumpup's latest masterpiece is the Stumpup 'Wallet Attack' white basketball boot with contrast trim. Leather and man-made upper. Padded tongue and collar. Rubber compound sole with attached balloons for extra lightness. Shock-absorbent. Just as well when we tell you the price.

£220.00

WINDOW ON THE STARS

The Hairdressers

Yet another mind-bogglingly wonderful, in-depth report by your very own roving investigative reporter, Mike Undernose.

'I've Combed the World for You', that catchy little number by the up and combing Hairdressers, is getting played non-stop in hair salons all over the place. 'It's lovely. The lead singer's got a lovely blow-wave. And the tune's so catchy. We snip in time to it,' explained Bruce from Choppers, Wood Green High Street.

So. Who are these newcomers, The Hairdressers? What is the secret of their success? I was determined to meet Adrian, Stacey, Gavin and Rita and find out for myself. Excitedly I took myself along to Hair Today Dye Tomorrow, Edmonton, where they all work. It was quite a relief to be going somewhere other than St Brat's, actually. Although, I must say I didn't really *want* a perm. But I suppose it's all part of the job. Us investigative reporters are fearless types who put up with anything for the sake of the job.

Anyway, the second I poked my nose around the door I was seized, bound about with towels, forced into a chair and set upon with shampoo. In moments I was head back in a sink, up to my eyes in lather. Not the most ideal way to conduct an interview, you might think. However, I managed to get in one question and one little joke before they wrapped my head in tin foil and high-baked me under a drier.

ME: Is 'I've Combed the World for You' your first single?

ADRIAN: Oh, no. We've cut two singles before. 'Short Back 'n' Sides' and 'Do You Want Your Roots Done?' They both flopped, actually.

ME: Not enough setting gel, perhaps? Ha, ha, ha.

ADRIAN: I don't think that's very funny, actually. Pass those scissors, Gavin, he's being cheeky. Short back and sides, wasn't it? Or how about a nice perm . . .

ME: Arrgh! Groo! Mercy! etc.

★ ★ ★ ★ ★ ★ ★ ★ ★ ★ ★

THE WORDS TO 'I'VE COMBED THE WORLD FOR YOU'

I've combed the world for you
I've had a brush with danger
I've tried out herb shampoo
On many a hapless stranger,

So pass the curlers, Joe,
And another glass of squash,
I only hope that everything
Will come out in the wash.

THE
FOLDS-OUT-INTO-A-HANDY-STOOL
GUITAR!

Guitarists! Do you get tired of standing on stage, waiting for your turn to do a solo? Do your legs ache from all that fancy footwork? Buy our strikingly stylish ozone friendly, versatile FOLDS-OUT-INTO-A-HANDY-STOOL GUITAR! The guitar is cleverly hinged, allowing you to either play it or sit on it, looking cool and laid back while you wait your turn for a solo. £81 only. You won't believe your eyes. Guaranteed for one year, providing you weigh under three stone.

✂ -

Yes! Please rush me my Folds-Out-Into-A-Handy-Stool Guitar without delay. I enclose my life's savings.

Name...

Address...

* Allow up to two years for delivery.

The Dads

– Is this true 'Pop' music?

'Sing An Embarrassing Song' is one of the most surprising chart hits of the last decade. Who would have thought that a corny outfit like The Dads would get to number 17?! Who do they appeal to? Who is buying this awful, cringe-making record? The mums, probably. *Trash Hits* went along to meet them. Father of three Mike is an accountant, and also the lead singer. Bearded dad of twins Ted works for the council and plays the accordion very, very badly. Stan has just got the one boy. He is between jobs and plays spoons. Father of five Bob is a bus driver and sings backing vocals while wearing a silly hat. Dad of triplets Arthur works in an office and writes the lyrics.

How Much 'Father' Can They Go?

How The Dads came up with the idea for their hit single

MIKE: Well, we were just sitting around one night over a pint, chatting about how we could best embarrass the kids, for a laugh, like. You said, 'Call the headmistress luv and blow pipesmoke in her face before stepping on her foot,' as I recall, Stan, ho, ho, ho.

STAN: Ha, ha, ha, that's right, Mike, so I did. And Ted here suggested 'Wearing Bermuda shorts to prize-giving', remember, Ted, ho, ho, ho?

TED: Ha, ha, ha, that I do. And Bob came up with something good. What was it again, Bob?

BOB: Heh, heh, heh. 'Boring all their friends with talking about what it were like in the old days when a tune was a tune and we were all chimney sweeps with nothing to eat but Hovis.'

MIKE: That was it, ha, ha, ha. But credit where it's due. It was Arthur here that came up with the song idea.

ARTHUR: That's right. I just happened to notice that if there's one thing that makes my kids cringe with embarrassment, it's me singing 'Catch a Falling Star'. Especially when I do the movements to go with it.

Strolling along pretending I have a microphone. That sort of thing.

MIKE: So straight away, we decided to go for it. Write a really embarrassing song, and record it. And that's how 'Sing an Embarrassing Song' came about.

TED: Arthur's already written the follow-up. It's called 'Fall Over in the Fathers' Race on Sports Day'.

STAN: All the other parents will love it, but the kids won't see the joke at all. What a hoot, eh?

– Catch The Dads on their forthcoming tour commencing Father's Day

'SING AN EMBARRASSING SONG'

(THE DADS)

(Yes – it's to the tune of 'John Brown's Body'!!)

If you want to show your children up
You really can't go wrong,
If you jump up on a table
And commence to sing a song
Wearing really silly trousers
Which are much too short (or long)
Or have flares that look all wrong.

Chorus
That's the way to show your kids up,
That's the way to show your kids up,
That's the way to show your kids up
Just sing an embarrassing song!

MATCH THE POP STAR TO THE PET

On the left are the pictures of six pop stars.
On the right are their pets. Can you match them?

THE STARS

Eric Stuffy

Wayne Swankpot

Roxanne Pebbles

The Cool Drooler

Trigger

Rita – Hairdresser

THE PETS

A Sample Fan Letter

Have you ever thought about sending a letter to your favourite pop star? Have you ever known what you want to say but can't get the words right on paper? Well, here is a handy cut-out-and-fill-in fan letter for idiots, which can be sent to the pop star of your choice.

Simply select the words of your choice from the following list and insert in the spaces.

Loaf of bread	Stamps
Wardrobe	Microscope
Lean beef	Fruit fly
Ball of wool	Brick

Ooops. Sorry, wrong list. Here is the right one:

brill	magic
ace	fab
fabsy, wabsy	guuuuurrreat
cute	handsome, charming smile

* *On second thoughts, the letter might be more interesting if you choose words from the first list.*

Dear <u>Big Bird</u>,

Both my friend and I think you are
utterly <u>Yellow</u> <u>with</u>,
<u>plenty</u>, <u>of</u>,
<u>bushy</u>, <u>feathers</u>
and <u>a big ?</u>.

With lots of love from

<u>ellipang</u>

(Sign your name)

P.S. You have a really <u>nice ?</u>

GREAT POP STARS OF OUR TIME:
Kit Spitt and the Gitts

by Morbid Lee Kurius

Kit Spitt
– angry ranting

Crazed Roy
– hammer and glass

Reg Raging
– comb and paper

Kit Spitt and the Gitts – recently voted 'The band you'd least like to spend a wet playtime with.'

Q: Let's start with you, Kitt. I understand your real name is Sonny Day.

KIT SPITT: OK, you lot, who told him? Who told him that? Well, that's just terrific. That makes me real fed up, that does. You just can't trust anyone. I'm leaving the band. Goodbye for ever. (Walks out of interview in huff.)

REG RAGING: He gets like that sometimes. It's all that deep anger!

CRAZED ROY: We're a very angry band, actually. In fact, I'm feeling really angry now. Excuse me, do you mind leaning back? I've got this compulsive urge to put my hammer through that window . .

ALBUMS
Rage (Cross Records)
Fury (Cross Records)
Total Annoyance (Cross Records)

SINGLES
'Hate! Grrrrr! Shut Up!' (Cross Records)

WORDS TO 'HATE! GRRRRR! SHUT UP!'

Arrrrrrgh! Yaaaaaaaaaah!
Hate! Hate! Grrrrrrrrrr!
Arrrrrrgh! Yaaaaaaaaaah!
Gerroff, gerroff, leemeurlone!
Shan't! Won't! Hate! Grrrrrr!
Shut Up! (baby)

JOKES

What do you call a man
with an electric plug
coming out of his head?
Mike.

What do drummers like
to eat?
Chicken drumsticks and cymbalina pudding.

Why was Samson the most popular pop star in the bible?
He brought the house down.

GUITAR: Will you go out with me?
VIOLIN: OK. But no strings attached.

What sort of trousers do piano players wear?
Cords.

If you had six bottles of lemonade, could you start a pop group?

Admiring Fan: How did you develop your powerful voice?
Singer: In our house, there wasn't a lock on the toilet door.

Heard about the new dance craze called the Lift?
It's got no steps.

Heard about the new dance craze called the Chimney?
It makes you get hot and puff a lot.

Heard about the new dance craze called the Happy Policeman?
It's got a nice beat.

Heard about the new dance craze called the Fridge?
It's real cool.

T-SHIRTS

HATE!
GRRRR!
SHUT UP!

I am a Dull
fan and prefer
plain grey
T-shirts with
no writing on

SHOCKING
BADDIES
4 EVER

BUY 3,
GET 1 FREE!

Other T-Shirts include

Stomachs are in, Chests are out
Cloth-Eared and Proud
My Other T-Shirt's a Suit
I'll Never Forget Thingy and the Other One
If Music Be the Food Of Love, Give Us a Bite of Your Maracas

THE DRIBBLES

FASCINATING FACTS

Everyone knows The Dribbles invented the very popular new dance craze, the Salivation, which is even now sweeping the country. Well, Mrs Ava Kneesup of St Austel claims to have mastered it, anyway. But here's a few facts you don't know!

♥ The Dribbles are all brothers, except for the girls, who are sisters!

♥ The eldest Dribble, Clint, likes to be known as the Cool Drooler!

♥ The Dribbles tried many names before they found the right one. At various times in their career they've been known as The Splatters, The Slurps and The Sploshies!

♥ Dribbles is better!

♥ Unless you're sitting in the front row at one of their concerts!

TRASH HITS CROSSWORD PUZZLE

Across

1. The yuckiest band around (13)
6. Watch out – she'll tell the teacher on you (6)
9. The Dads are definitely over the —— (4)
10. One of The Dull (4)
11. One of The Dads could be called this (3)
12. A Dinner Lady (4)
13. Wayne Swankpot knows he is one (3)
14. A Shocking Baddy (3)

Down

1. The band you may not want to meet after school (8)
2. One of The Cutesy Pies (8)
3. He has a country corner (9)
4. You may feel this after eating a Dinner Ladies meal (3)
5. Wayne ———— is beautiful! (8)
7. The oldest band in the business? (4)
8. Another Dinner Lady (3)

Answers on page 123

HEAVY METAL

Shy, retiring types who are always asking if you could 'turn that music down, please, I've a bit of a headache'. (Ho, ho, ho. Just our little joke.)

Image: Oh, hairy. You've definitely got to have the hair. Tattoos, nails through the nose, ripped jackets, tight trousers and crazed werewolf earrings are nothing unless you've got the hair. Us heavy metal types do a lot of hair tossing. Our hair is very important to us. Some of us keep small animals in it.

Hang-out: Garages, especially ones with motor bikes in. The top of high cliffs, so we can jump off for a laugh and not get hurt, because we're so incredibly tough.

Favourite food: Anything tough and greasy. My particular favourite is cuff-off-a-leather-jacket, deep-fried in sump oil. Not everyone likes that.

Likes: Noise. Oh, the delight of a revving motor bike first thing in the morning! The joy of strolling in the park one Sunday and unexpectedly hearing a lesser-spotted pneumatic drill. If there's one thing we can't stand, it's peace and quiet. We think peace and quiet's cissy.

Dislikes: Bands with names like The Tiptoeing Pixies. Birdwatching, because you have to be quiet.

Illnesses: We don't get ill. We're too tough. Apart from the occasional dose of drummer's elbow or guitarist's ankle, we rarely bother the doctor. We do a bit of friendly wrestling, just to keep ourselves fit. We believe that a grapple a day keeps the doctor away.

Remedy: What, for drummer's elbow? Oh, six months total rest in the Bahamas should do the trick.

Ambition: To be the noisiest band in the multiverse.

COUNTRY

Stetsons, chaps, boots, blue and white checked shirts, pigtails and gingham smocks – and that's just the horses! Tend to shout 'Ya hoo!' at the slightest provocation. Have spurs that jingle, jangle, jingle as they go riding merrily along.

Image: Cowboys. Eh? Oh, sorry, I mean cowpersons. We like to give the impression there ain't nothin' we don't know about cows. Even if the nearest we've ever gotten to one is scoffin' a milk chocolate bar, haw haw, ya hoo! If I had to pick one item of clothing that kinda typifies us poor simple country folk, I guess it'd be expensive boots. And I ain't talkin' about the kinda boots you'd be happy to trail through cow pooh neither. I'm talkin' big bucks. You need to buy a special cream, that kinda thang.

Hang-out: Home, home on the range where the deer and the antelope play. Or preferably the Loaded Texan Hotel.

Favourite food: Beans. Eaten on a tin plate under the stars. Before going back to the Loaded Texan for a four-course meal with double helpings of apple pie and cream and after dinner mints. Ya hoo!

Likes: Cows. Fiddles. Country dancing, where someone shouts out instructions:
Swing that girl in a dozy do,
Crash your boot down on her toe,
ya hoo! etc.

Dislikes: Those rough saloon bars with half-sized doors that swing back and knock you in the butt. Like Sleezy Sal's place. I wouldn't wear a decent pair of boots in there, I can tell you.

Illnesses: Sore bums from being photographed sitting on horses all day.

Remedy: A cushion.

Ambition: To star in a Western with Lil Orphant Annie.

OPERA

(Well, it's popular with some people, isn't it?)

Operatic types are usually big, with big names to match, like Antibiotica Von Constabulari, Plasticine De Bingo, Kurri Te Takaway, Scrachalotti, etc. They have big chests, big tummies and big voices. Singing at the top of your voice burns up calories, and they have big appetites. It usually costs big money to go and hear them.

Image: Depends on the opera. We wear whatever the part calls for. But you can bet your life that big bottoms in huge pairs of tights and humungus frocks with plunging necklines will crop up somewhere along the line.

Hang-out: We're never far from the stage. We often have parties there after the final curtain-call. The whole cast gathers to carouse on champagne and twiglets and the odd boar's head. You can hear the stage groaning under the combined weight of us all. Sometimes it gives way altogether. That's what we opera singers call 'going through a stage'.

Favourite food: Ah. Well, personally I always like to start with *oeufs-en-cocotte*, which is eggs in individual ramekins, each set on a bed of diced ham, bacon and chicken livers. I tend to follow this with *feuillets de fruits de mer aux epinards*, which is basically prawns in puff pastry served with spinach . . . (deleted, owing to lack of space)

Likes: Singing. Eating. In that order. Or maybe the other way round.

Dislikes: Getting the part of the gruff old grandfather or the nurse, where you sing one line (such as oh ho, ho, ho), then exit and are never seen again.

Illnesses: Sore throats from screaming secrets at the top of our voices.

Remedy: A scarf at all times and gargling frequently with chocolate biscuits.

Ambition: A starring role in a good, long-drawn-out death scene.

RAP

Very cool dressers who wear a lot of gold and can only speak in rhythmic verse. Tend to boast a bit, but who can blame them? So would you if you could afford wicked designer sneakers, which instantly transform you into a ba–a–d, trend-settin', seriously awesome top-fashion leader, kno' wot I mean?

Image: You talkin' to me? Sure, I got style
Hold a fashion competition
And I'll win it by a mile
Cos I got the looks,
I got the class
And I learnt it from a camel
In the Khyber Pass. *[Ed. Surely some mistake?]*

Hang-out: Out on the street,
That's where we meet,
Just groovin' on down
To the funky beat.

Favourite food: We got the time for food that rhymes
We don't like bananas but we do like limes
We don't like artichokes cos they're too hard
We don't like butter but we quite like lard.
[Ed. Are you absolutely sure about this?]

Likes: Words that rhyme
Every time.

Dislikes: Words that don't
Get our goat(??)

Illnesses: Tonsilitis, sinusitis,
Adenoids and chilblains,
Belly-ache and chicken-pox,
Fainting clean away,
Bad cold, skin rash,
Breakin' out in pimples
Many are the illnesses
That come a rapper's way.

Remedy: Gotta see the doctor,
Gotta see the nurse,
Gotta get some medicine
To stop me gettin' worse.

Ambition: To end this rap
And take a little nap.

MATCH THE POP STAR TO THE SHOE

On the left are some pictures of pop stars. On the right are some pictures of their shoes. Can you match them up?

THE SHOES

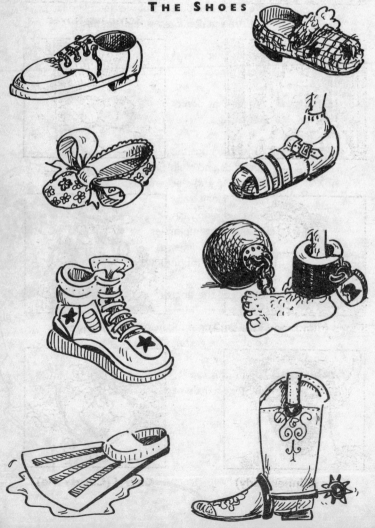

I.C. Cool

Rambling Rover

Jay L. Bait

Roxanne Pebbles

Clifford Mundane (The Dull)

Roy Rodgers

Vera (Dinner Lady)

Cheryl (Cutesy Pie)

Results of Readers' Poll

Spottiest Saxophonist ☆ Brad Acne

Worst Male Singer in World ☆ Tony Def

Worst Female Singer In World ☆ May Q. Wince

Loudest Drummer ☆ Ed Ake

Biggest Male Show-Off ☆ Luke Atme

Biggest Female Show-Off ☆ Mega Lomania

Best Pianist ☆ Doody Fiddleybits

Worst Pianist ☆ Des Cordant

Worst Guitarist ☆ Orville Twanging

Best Mouth Organ Players ☆ Justin Hale and Den Blowout

WHAT'S ON

Mon 4 May

THE DINNER LADIES –
hot from the stove!

Tues 5

From the USA –
THE BURGERKINGS

Wed 6

THE PLUMPS

Thurs 7

From Scotland –
**ROCKIN' JOCK AND THE
HOT HAGGIS HEADS**

Fri 8

MAIN COURSE AND AFTERS

Sat 9

Special appearance –
THE THREE LITTLE PIGS

Sun 10

Your old favourite –
CHIP BUTTY

✪ ✪ ✪

THE CANTEEN

✪ ✪ ✪ ✪ ✪ ✪ ✪ ✪

**12 Nosh Road
London T42**

✪ ✪ ✪ ✪ ✪ ✪ ✪ ✪

THE CANTEEN

109

Share your agony

with Dr Cressida Callous

Gotta problem? No one to tell your troubles to? Write for advice to *Trash Hits'* very own problem expert. Famous for her no-nonsense approach, Dr Callous goes where no other agony doctor has gone before. None of this sympathy lark. Bedside manner? Forget it.

HER BUNGED-UP NOSE

Dear Dogtor,
Wad cad be dud if subbody suffers frob a bugged ub doze all de tibe? By de way, I ab talkig aboud by wife, dod me. Dere is nothig rog wid by doze. I just cand spell.

Bad Speller, Portsmouth

The Doc replies:
Take poison three times a day before meals.

CAREER WORRY

Dear Doctor,
My parents want me to be a prawnbroker. However, I want to be a piano tuna and crab a little happiness while I can. Is this shellfish?

A. Lobster, St Ives, Cornwall

The Doc replies:
My, my. Dig that crazy crustacean. I really do get 'em sometimes. Watch out for the post, A. Lobster, your strait-jacket is on its way.

LOONY RELATIVE

Dear Doctor,
My sister sleeps under the bed. I think she's a little potty.

Lorna Grub, Somerset

The Doc replies:
You think you've got problems? My uncle thought he was a toilet. I confronted him about it and he flushed. Don't waste my time.

FEARFUL FOR HAIR

Dear Doctor,
I am a glamorous pop star and need to look my best. Grooming is so important, don't you think? Tired of my lank locks, I sent away for a bottle of Len's Lizard Oil, the wonder shampoo from South America. Since using it, my hair has come alive. See enclosed photo. As a woman of science, do you think I should carry on using it?

Medusa, Walton-on-the-Nez

The Doc replies:
Snakes alive! Don't use it again, it's probably pythonous!

HE JUST CAN'T HELP IT

Dear Doctor,
Is it just me, or are there any other compulsive writers of boring letters to magazines out there? I am trying to stop myself doing this, but I just can't help it. My hand just automatically reaches out every time I see a pencil.

Mustapha Stamp, Milton Keynes

The Doc replies:
Mustapha, you are not alone. There are many other idiots like you. Contact the National Association for Compulsive Writers of Boring Letters to Magazines (NACWBLM) about your problem and stop writing to me about it. In the mean time, if you feel the urge coming on again, staple your hand to the table. A simple but effective solution.

A-Z OF POP MUSIC

A – **Acne.** Dreaded ultra-oozy spots. Sometimes found on pop stars. It is difficult to be alluring if your face looks like an eruption on the surface of Neptune. Sadly, acne is very difficult to cure. Try cutting your head off, when the condition will mysteriously vanish all by itself. (See Z for Zits.)

B – **Blues.** Something you sing. Not to be confused with greens, which are something you eat. Or oranges, which are occasionally used as snowman noses.

C – **Conceited.** What pop stars become when all the fame and adoration and tons of fan mail and riding in limousines and gifts of lugworm dressing-gowns gets too much for them. (See W for Wayne Swankpot.)

D – **Drum solo**. The bit where the drummer goes unrestrainably bonkers among the cymbals for a very long time, while the rest of the band wander off to have a sleep/cup of tea/quiet read/chat, etc.

E – **Eric Stuffy**. Bass player with The Dull. Edits the *Slug Fanciers'* weekly. Wants to own a slug farm one day.

F – **Fan mail.** Drooly letters in a sack. Often plastered with yucky lipstick and SWALK (Slapped With a Lukewarm Kipper). Usually soggy with tear stains.

G – **Guitar.** Popular six-stringed instrument. Not to be confused with catarrh, which is yucky stuff up your nose.

H – **Hair style.** Most pop stars have one. The sillier the style, the higher the street cred.

I – **Idol.** As in 'He Is My Idol' i.e. favourite, much-adored and admired person. Not to be confused with idle. As in 'He Is Idle' i.e. lazy layabout who lies in bed playing guitar. (Often, of course, He Is Both.)

J – **Jam session.** Could mean a group of musicians getting together to make a terrible racket. Or could mean a group of greedy pigs getting together to stuff their faces with jammy doughnuts, etc. If you get the choice, go for the doughnuts.

K – **Kayak.** Eskimo canoe, probably used to transport Eskimo pop stars and their equipment from one ice-flow to another. Well, maybe.

L – **La.** The note that follows soh, as pointed out in that famous song that begins 'Doe a deer, a female deer'. Also useful for singers who forget the words. (La, la, la, la, la, etc.)

M – **Music**. Something never ever played by the likes of The Shocking Baddies or Kit Spitt and the Gitts.

N – **Number One**. The pinnacle of success. This is what all pop stars are striving towards. Doesn't necessarily mean the song is any good, of course. Unless you happen to like warmed-up wellies.

O – **Oranges**. Juicy, acid fruit often used to make snowman noses. Not to be confused with Blues, which you sing, or greens, which you eat. (See B for Blues.)

P – **Pop**. What the weasel went. Also short for popular, as in 'Popular Music'. Odd. You wouldn't have thought an exploding weasel would be very popular, would you?

Q – Questions that pop stars hate being asked. Like 'Have you ever thought of taking guitar lessons?'

R – **Rhythm**. What The Dull have not got.

S – **Star**. What Wayne Swankpot knows he is. What Thingy and the Other One would like to be. What Mrs Sonia Bladder, an eighty-year-old retired traffic warden from Newcastle, will never be. (Although you can never be sure – think of the The Dinner Ladies.)

T – **Truly**. Useful word used by pop stars to put in front of other words, e.g. 'Truly Awful' when asked about someone else's record or 'Truly Amazing' when asked about their own.

U – **Ugh!** Expression of disgust or horror uttered when first laying eyes upon a plate of food cooked by The Dinner Ladies.

V – **Vibes**. As in 'Dig Those Crazy'. Archaic, hippy way of saying 'I say, this music is jolly good, eh wot?'

W – **Wayne Swankpot**. A pop star who is so vain he thinks he actually deserves three mentions in the A to Z of pop music.

X – **Xebec**. Small three-masted Mediterranean vessel with square sails, nothing whatsoever to do with pop music. Ha, ha. Bet you thought it'd be Xylophone!

Y – **Yes**. What you say when offered an awful lot of money to make a pop song.

Z – **Zits**. We started with acne and we end with zits. What could be nicer? Happy squeezing.

Your Horoscope

LIBRA

Something exciting is about to happen, so be alert. Lerts are fun-loving little creatures with a natural sense of rhythm. You'll have more fun being a Lert than aggressive, I can tell you. Gressives tend to get into fights and hum tunelessly for hours on end.

SCORPIO

Be cautious this week. If you meet a one-armed man, give him a hand. Beware of violinists who might be on the fiddle. Take care of your health. Have your eyes ever been checked? Or have they always been striped?

SAGITTARIUS

You have time on your hands. Now is as good a time as any to learn a musical instrument. Remember. No matter what people tell you, a triangle is not square. If you don't get on with that, try carpentry. Make a bandstand – take away their chairs.

CAPRICORN

You are in a wild and reckless mood at the moment. It's a good week for little jokes. Enjoy yourself. Find someone carrying a large double-bass and laughingly say, 'Bet you can't get that under your chin.' Then duck. Alternatively, carry a miniature goal-post in your pocket and keep taking it out and asking people for a match.

AQUARIUS

Talking of jokes, have you looked in the mirror lately? Obviously not. The time has come for a complete change of image. Let your clothes reflect your mood. Be cool. Wear a fridge on your head. Or be flashy and wear a lighthouse. Or be totally wet and wear a tap.

PISCES

Mercury, your planetary sign, is in Taurus, but this planet is locking itself into confrontation with Pluto, which in turn is challenging Neptune. None of this means anything whatsoever, but is a very good way of filling up space. In the mean time, avoid falling hair – step to one side.

ARIES
Don't expect too much. Remember, eggs and paving stones are not all they're cracked up to be. And Donald Duck isn't all he's quacked up to be. It's a bad time for losing things. If you can't find the M6, drive up the M3 twice.

TAURUS
The guitarists among you shouldn't be afraid to pull a few strings. Drummers are in for a thumping good time.

GEMINI
You will feel nostalgic and remember old friends. Names will come out of the past to haunt you. Quasimodo. Does

that name ring a bell? Or Frank Foot, who was a leg-end in his own life time?

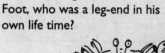

CANCER
If at first you don't succeed, probably best not try sky-diving.

LEO
You will get out of bed, break your ankle, lose your money, fall down a well and spend six weeks in hospital. But cheer up. Remember, if it wasn't for Venetian blinds, it'd be curtains for all of us.

VIRGO
Be a ringleader. Get in the bath first. Oh, and you can expect a windfall. The fates do not reveal what form this will take, but knowing your luck, the chances are a large, hard, maggoty cooking-apple will fall directly on your head. Have a nice week, and remember – hippies keep your leggies on !

Song Lyrics

'THE TORN TROUSER BLUES'

(Wild Man Throttle)

Woke up this mornin'
Fell off my bike,
Yeah, woke up this mornin', babe,
Fell off my bike,
Ripped my new pants, babe,
Rather more than I'd like.

Chorus
I got them torn trouser blues,
Got them torn trouser blues,
Oh, oh, woe is me
Sure got them torn trouser blues.

Got to my feet, yeah,
Felt kinda blue
Felt kinda blue, babe,
Well, wouldn't you?
Cos I stepped in some dog do
Got it over my shoe.

Got them dirty shoe blues, etc.

I walked to some grass, babe,
Just to get my shoe clean
Yeah, I walked to some grass, girl
To get my shoe clean
And that grass was a swamp, girl,
If you know what I mean.

Got them goin' under blues, etc.

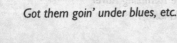

'TRA LA LA, TRA LA LA, TRA LA LANDY'

(The Rambling Rover)

If I sing about flowers
I can bore you for hours,
Tra la la, tra la la, tra la landy,
If I sing about trees
You'll be down on your knees
Tra la la, tra la la,
You'll be bandy.

I can sing about leprechauns,
Bunnies and clover,
My rambling ballads are
Never soon over,
And that's why they call me the Rambling Rover
Tra la, tra la la, tra la landy.

'TELLING THE TEACHER ON YOU'

(Sandra and the Snitches)

I'm telling the teacher on you
I seen what you done with the glue,
Don't try to deny it cos I know it's true
I'm telling the teacher on you.

Chorus
Oooooh, what a sneak,
Oooooh, what a sneak,
Oooooh, what a sneak is that Sandra.

I'm gonna tell Miss what you did,
I seen what you carved on the lid,
I wouldn't keep quiet if you gave me a quid,
I'm gonna tell Miss what you did.

Chorus
Oooooh, what a sneak,
Oooooh, what a sneak,
Oooooh, what a sneak is that Sandra.

'A masterpiece' – *Toytown Times*

'A wonderfully rich and resonant piece
of video-making' – Postman Pat

'A classic' – Rupert Bear

Classified

PERSONAL

Complainers fan, shy, sensitive, spotty, poetic, seeks friend.

Nobody understands me,
Why I cannot see,
Would you like to come on round
And hear my poetreee?
No?
Oh well . . .
Box no. 347

I am a Dull fan and I wish to meet others like me. I am into waiting in queues and reading books about extractor fans. Come on over, and we'll examine my fascinating collection of Yale keys over a glass of tap water. Box no. 123

WANTED

Experienced comb and paper player required for The Hairdressers (whose hit single, 'I Combed the World for You', has reached number 29). Ring Gavin on 356 8649 (salon hours only).

Vocalist wanted. King Kong lookalike wanted for duets with Quasimodo lookalike. Together, let's show 'em the real meaning of stage fright! Photo please. Box no. 508

Bass wanted for sole band. No old trouts or rock salmon need apply. Ring Tina Tuna, 795 2222.

Wanted. Heavy Metal fan. Mine's made of cardboard, and keeps blowing over. Ring 354 25073 and ask for Mr Barmy.

MESSAGES

Will Cynthia Sizer please contact Terry O'Fonick.

Baa Lamb. Me 'n' Ewe for ever, babe. Hunky Sheep.

FOR SALE

■ The complete works of The Dull. Help! If I hear them one more time, I'll turn into a brick or a cabbage leaf or something as boring as that. A box, even. Box no. 243.

RECORDS WANTED

■ Top prices. All old records bought, except for the complete works of The Dull, which if played too often will make you turn into a brick or a cabbage leaf or something as boring as that. A box, perhaps. Ring 123 and ask for Big Ben.

FAN CLUB NEWS

■ Dinner Ladies Fans annual dinner, to be held at St Brat's on Wednesday at 12 sharp. Formal overalls only. Make sure your hands are clean and say please when you ask for an autograph. No seconds. No pushing in the queue. *Bon appetit!*

TUITION

■ Learn to sing with the acclaimed greatest voice trainer Costiou Alotti! 'I gotta ways of makin' you heeta the high notes.'

FOUND

■ One pair of glasses.

COMPLAINT

■ Please print larger – I've lost my glasses.

ANSWERS TO CROSSWORD PUZZLE ON PAGE 97

Across. 1. The Cutesy Pies
6. Sandra 9. Hill 10. Eric
11. Dad 12. Vera 13. Hit
14. Kev

Down. 1. Teachers
2. Charlene 3. Snakejack
4. Ill 5. Swankpot 7. Dads
8. Lil

THE CHARTS:

TRASH HITS' BOTTOM 25 SINGLES

26 **Dangerous Waters**
Roxanne Pebbles and the Odd Shark (Fish)

27 **Who's Been Telling Porkies?**
Eliza Lott (Nark)

28 **Ever Been Inside?**
Jay L. Bait (Pokey Records)

29 **I've Combed the World for You**
The Hairdressers (Snip Records)

30 **Yeah, Yeah, Yeah!**
The Repetitions (Ditto)

31 **Throw Another Log Cabin on the Fire**
Roy Rodgers and Trigger (Hoss Records)

32 **Tra La La, Tra La La, Tra La Landy**
The Rambling Rover (Green)

33 **Yodelling Song**
Hans Neeson-Bumpsadaisy (Old Hat)

34 **A Good Day for Washing**
Dry Dry Dry (Soap Sounds)

35 **I'm a Really Useful Person**
Ann D. Windsor (Majestic Sounds)

36 **Across the Sea**
Olive Abroad (Faraway Records)

37 **Tug o' War**
Paul de Rope (Heave Records)

38 **You Can't Hurry Love**
Ena Tick and Arthur Mo (Jiffy Records)

39 **Stay in at Playtime**
The Teachers (Chalk Records)

40 **I Wanna Be Your Butler**
Urang Urang (Bowtie Records)

41 **Missing You**
Eva Sy and Philippa Hanky (Kleenex)

42 **We've Fallen Out**
Sella Field (Greenogram)

43 **The Northern Line Blues**
The Tube (Cross)

44 **The Torn Trouser Blues**
Wild Man Throttle (Blush)

45 **We've Got a Lot of Catching Up to Do**
Bea Hynd (Old Hat)

46 **Not Another Monday**
Sunday Night Blues Singers (Kleenex)

47 **You've Set My Love Alight**
The Firefighters (Breeze Records)

48 **Hey! You! Get Offa My Chair!**
The Three Bears (Bruin Records)

49 **Deep Sea Blues**
The Snorkels (Fish)

50 **Falling For You**
Humphrey Dumtee (Old Hat)